BASEBALL STRENGTH 101

by CJ Appenzeller

TABLE OF CONTENTS

Chapter 1: The Strength Training Myth

Strength training is the most overlooked and underrated tool in the baseball player's toolbox to help him improve performance and stay on the field. This book is going to give you an inside look at why strength training is important for ballplayers, the impact it can have, and finally a sneak peek at what's needed to make up a great strength training program for a baseball player.

Misconceptions about Strength Training

Here at my gym, Appenzeller Training Systems, we have had huge successes helping baseball athletes improve their performance and stay healthy and resilient all season long. However, even with our great track record, we still frequently hear misconceptions and myths among parents, coaches, and players surrounding baseball and strength training.

The first big myth is that strength training is going to make players bulky or will slow them down. Another one is that it will throw off a guy's swing or mess with his arm slot for throwing. Essentially, these concerns have to do with the idea that strength training could get in the way of a player's skill development and make him worse on the field. Some of the other ones I've heard are that strength training will increase the risk of injury, strength training will make guys too sore to play or practice, and—this is a big one—that working with resistance bands alone is enough strength training to keep a player strong and healthy for baseball.

Really, these notions couldn't be further from the truth.

STRENGTH TRAINING AND BULK

This is a common myth that's been passed down from generation to generation. I know that back in the day in baseball, strength training was greatly frowned upon. If you were an old-time player and you did any type of strength training, you were definitely the exception to the rule.

The problem is this: guys see bodybuilders and power lifters on the internet, and they think, "Man, if I looked like that, I don't know if I'd be able to compete at a high level of baseball." What they're missing is the fact that those guys who look that way—bodybuilders, power lifters, guys with really huge muscles—work extremely hard to achieve that physique in a much different way than a baseball player should be training.

So the training methodologies are totally separated from one another. Guys just aren't going to get that big and that bulky without training that way, without a certain type of diet, a certain type of supplementation, and also without having a laser focus on being that big. Baseball players should have their laser focus on improving their skills, number one, and then on improving their strength and explosive power to aid in the improvement of those skills. Not necessarily on gaining excessive muscle.

STRENGTH TRAINING PREVENTS INJURY

The number-one benefit any baseball player is going to get from proper strength training is injury prevention. Strength training is going to open up the ability for guys to stay on the field longer. Baseball is a game in which injury is becoming more and more common. We've all heard this before. We are seeing injuries at even the youngest levels, the youth ranks, things like Little Leaguer's elbow, that you never even heard about until recently. Then there are tears of the UCL, the "Tommy John ligament" as it's called, and rotator cuff tears that are all commonplace for youth baseball players.

All of these injuries are extremely common in kids, even kids as young as 12 or 13 years old, because they're playing so much baseball and they're not taking the time to develop their musculature, to develop those movements in the proper way that will keep them on the field. So injury prevention would be the number-one benefit anyone can expect to get from proper strength training.

STRENGTH TRAINING INCREASES POWER

On top of injury prevention, strength training can do a whole lot more. The primary appeal of strength training to the players is that it increases their power. So if you're a hitter, you're going to increase the distance you can hit the ball. You're going to increase the likelihood that you're driving the ball gap to gap with every at-bat. And you're going to increase the likelihood that you can hit the ball a long way. With strength training, you're really increasing bat speed and bat power, explosive power with the bat in your hands.

Strength training also helps you maximize your velocity. If you're a thrower, you want to throw harder, whether you're a pitcher or a position player. Proper strength training is absolutely going to maximize your velocity or how hard you can throw. It's going to maximize the distance you can throw. It's going to maximize the number of guys you throw out at home plate from the outfield. It's going to maximize the close plays that go your way in the infield, and it's also going to add miles per hour on the pitcher's mound.

One final element is that you're going to be able to increase your speed through proper strength training. That means speed home to first, that means speed on the base path, that means first steps to balls, getting a little greater range in the outfield, getting a little greater range in the infield. Also, a base runner will get more stolen bases. So all of that stuff can be improved through strength training. It's just a matter of doing the right things at the right time throughout the season and doing it with the right person.

WHAT TO EXPECT WITHOUT STRENGTH TRAINING

If a young athlete doesn't participate in strength training, there may be some negative consequences in his game. Here's what parents, players, and coaches can expect when they don't include baseball as a part of their yearly preparation plan:

Number one is one that we've already mentioned—you can expect overuse injuries. Constantly playing the game of baseball is going to beat up certain muscles. Certain areas of the body are going to be susceptible to the constant wear and tear. Strength training helps prevent overuse of the areas and prepares players to be more resilient, thus leading to less injury.

Second is that, without strength training, you can expect a higher rate of burnout. Guys at a young age that are playing competitive sports, especially baseball, get into competition so young now. There are 8U travel teams, for instance, that are going from tournament to tournament every weekend. If you're constantly playing a sport over and over and over again, week in and

INCREASING POWER AND HITTING THE BALL FURTHER

We've had guys come to us as singles hitters, great contact guys who consistently make contact and hit for a high average become league leaders in double and triples. The power development benefit for hitters from strength training, when done properly, is HUGE. Specifically, I know one of our guys, Tyler, was a slash hitter his sophomore season in high school. He got playing time on varsity, but he simply couldn't make it happen with his bat and couldn't drive in runners. After his sophomore year, he dedicated himself to training with our program consistently and doing every little thing I asked of him. By the end of his junior year, he was hitting doubles and triples regularly and was in the starting lineup for his high school. THIS is what an increase in power can do for a baseball player—get him IN the lineup and blow his numbers UP.

week out—yes, a lot of guys love to play and to play competitively—it gets to a certain point where you can be burned out by the time you get to high school. I've seen 13- and 14-year-old kids who don't want to play baseball anymore because that's all they've done. They want to try other things, they want to play other sports. Maybe they don't want to play sports at all because they're just burned out on competition.

Strength training adds another element to the mix. It adds a new facet of competition. It adds a new way to improve yourself and push yourself and challenge yourself, day in and day out, week in and week out, which is going to mean you're less likely to get burned out.

Finally, without strength training, higher skilled players can expect minimum increase in their actual physical capabilities. If a player is extremely skilled, regardless of his age—without further increasing his strength and explosive capabilities, it will be extremely hard for him to maximize all of the skill potential he has and add things like velocity and bat speed. Skill work is number one, but it will only take you so far in regard to how much power you have with the bat and how hard you can throw. A marriage of strength training and skill training is what creates dominant ballplayers.

Player Showcase: Dhillon Barbetti

"From the first workout, my confidence grew in EVERY aspect of MY LIFE!"

After just a couple of months of training at ATS, I have become more flexible, my velocity has increased, and I've been so explosive throughout all my workouts. I was taught great form, and I learned how to breathe properly. I learned to stretch every night and to roll out too. I came into ATS doing kettlebell swings and struggling with 35 pounds. With the help of CJ and the team at ATS, I now crush the 100-pound kettlebell with great form. My squat went up more than 40 pounds, and my single-leg reverse lunge went up more than 15 pounds. My deadlift sprouted more than 20 pounds, and I can bust out 30 push-ups easily, when before, 15 to 20 was a struggle, and it wasn't even good form. I could barely do 10 pull-ups, and ATS has pushed me to get a 32-pull-up max.

From even the first workout at ATS, my confidence grew in every aspect of life. The work in the gym at ATS prepares me for all the challenges life and baseball throw at me—in the box before a pitch, at home, and even in school. ATS has showed me with time, attacking any set in life, and setting high goals, anything can be accomplished.

My favorite memory at ATS was a Saturday morning in August, a 9:30 session, and it was YAM's (James') last day before he went off for his last year at La Salle. It was already 80 degrees, but CJ shut the garage and back door and cranked the heat up before the warm-up even started. The session was intense, and just when you felt like giving up or slowing down, CJ would yell, "Who's gonna be the hardest worker in this room?" After that day, I truly saw the definition of a grind, and I realized that every day should be better than the day before. He gave us a sticker to remember that day, and I have that sticker in my car. When I see it, I look back to remind myself how hard I should be going each and every day.

—*Dhillon Barbetti*

Shore Regional High School Baseball

Player Showcase: Ben Hoffman

"ATS is the reason I'm playing Division I baseball today."

ATS is the reason I am playing Division I baseball today. The first day I walked through that door, I was a skinny 16-year-old kid who could barely pick up a barbell, let alone put any weights on it. ATS made me physically stronger, which in turn let my baseball skills take off to the next level.

Mentally, the training has taught me a whole new level of discipline. Training at ATS makes any workout you go through with your team seem simple in comparison. The blue collar mindset has taught me that in order to experience the results I want physically and on the baseball field, I need to show up to the gym every day ready to grind no matter what.

—*Ben Hoffman*
Monmouth University Baseball

CHAPTER 2: BASEBALL INJURIES

As we've talked about, baseball injuries are becoming more and more prevalent at a young age. Let's look at some of these specific injuries and talk about how strength training can help prevent them.

UCL TEAR (TOMMY JOHN)

If you've ever been around baseball, you've heard of players having to have "Tommy John surgery." But what is that? What exactly are you getting repaired when you have that surgery?

The Tommy John injury occurs when a player tears his ulnar collateral ligament (UCL). This ligament is located on the inner side of each elbow. The primary cause of a UCL tear is overuse. Constantly beating up the arm, pitching lots of innings— we see high inning totals with guys who tear this ligament. And then the process of coming back from this injury is something that is very, very scary for pitchers.

At my facility, we've dealt with tons of guys coming back from Tommy John surgery, and that's unfortunate. Many young players only come to us after they've had the surgery, after they've already torn the ligament, and they want to get back to the mound throwing better than ever. So it's a lengthy process. It takes about a year before you can start throwing again. The standard procedure is that it takes 11 months of healing and therapy before you can even pick up a baseball again, and it's 13 to 16 months before you're back in a game pitching. And of course, it's different for every individual. It depends on how you come through the surgery, it depends on your rehab, and it depends on what kind of shape you were in before.

Strength Training and Tommy John

Is there a way to reduce your chances of tearing your UCL? Yes! There are two very important ways to minimize your risk of a UCL tear. First is to keep your innings total down. Throw a little bit less, especially competitively off the mound. If I could give an ideal recommendation of throwing volume, I'd choose to only have our guys throw eight to nine months out of the year, and at a bare minimum, have guys take six weeks per year off with completely no throwing.

The second way to help avoid Tommy John surgery is to train with proper strength training with your strength coach. Strength training in general will do a little bit to help decrease the risk of Tommy John. Strength training is simply going to take you out of that loaded overuse pattern that throwing a baseball places the UCL in. Throwing is the fastest motion in all sports. The arm goes through something like 7,000 degrees of internal rotation in one second. Any kind of strength training is going to be almost totally the polar opposite from this, so it's going to allow you to load in a different way. It's going to allow you to avoid overuse.

There are several much more specific ways that strength training helps, though. When we see guys who have had a UCL tear, who have had Tommy John surgery, we see three things. The first is poor scapular function, or poor function of the shoulder

A TOMMY JOHN STORY

One of our college guys, James, came to us originally after his senior year of high school and after coming back from a torn Tommy John ligament. I'll never forget, the FIRST day he was cleared for training post-op, he was back in the gym with us and I remember thinking, thank God he's here with us and not somewhere else without proper supervision this early post-operation and coming back from a major surgery. Yam, as we call James around the gym, became one of the hardest-working athletes to ever step through our door, and he still owns several records here at the facility for his lower body strength and power. He stayed consistent and worked his ass off to achieve more than he had ever done. Through his training, he gained a sense of confidence in his arm and a sense of confidence in himself—he tells me all the time about a certain feeling of calm he gets when on the mound now that he never had before because he knows he's done the right things to get his arm back and his body stronger, bigger, and more powerful than ever before. Strength training helped Yam gain something we can't really see on a piece of paper—his CONFIDENCE and SWAGGER. I guess the fact that he now throws over 90 miles per hour doesn't hurt either!

blade. When your shoulder blade doesn't function properly, it has been shown to have a really big carry-over to developing a UCL tear in the future.

The second issue is poor rotator cuff strength. Even though the rotator cuff is in the shoulder, the Tommy John ligament, which is in the elbow, is downstream. If your rotator cuff is weak, that load is going to be disproportionately placed on the elbow.

The third issue is anterior core stability, or just plain "core strength," as most people know it. If you can't remain in certain positions and don't have the stability to be strong when your arm is over your head and stay neutral in your spine, it's going to be very, very hard to displace forces, and again we'll wind up with disproportionate force on the elbow.

So to put it all in a nutshell, three things that you want to train to make sure you decrease the risk of a Tommy John injury are:

- Scapular (shoulder blade) function

- Rotator cuff strength

- Anterior core strength

ROTATOR CUFF INJURY

That brings us to the rotator cuff. Again, there are specific ways to address the risk of a rotator cuff injury through strength training.

There are four rotator cuff muscles, and any one of those (or more) can get torn, so a rotator cuff injury tends to be individual to each person. Just like the UCL tear, the rotator cuff injury is an overuse injury. It happens to guys who pitch a lot of innings. The causes of this injury and the way you train to prevent it are very, very similar to what we talked about with the UCL, or the Tommy John injury.

STRENGTH TRAINING AND ROTATOR CUFF

First is the core stability. Second is the function of the scapula, or shoulder blade. And third, you want to make sure your throwing mechanics are solid. This may seem counterintuitive, but a lot of rotator cuff injuries come from guys with poor hip mobility. Basically, what happens is when you're throwing, you're jumping off one leg while you're moving your arm. Poor hip mobility causes that arm to take more stress, so you have more and disproportionate stress on the rotator cuff.

Those are the issues that we address when to make sure to avoid that rotator cuff strain or tear. And remember, overuse is the key. If you can cut down the number of innings you're playing or throwing throughout the year and increase the amount of strength training or general physical preparedness you're doing, then you'll drastically cut down the risk of that injury.

HIP INJURIES

A lot of professional baseball players have had issues with their hips. And even young kids, as they get bigger and stronger, have hip injuries. Like the rotator cuff, hip injuries can involve sev-

INNINGS VS. PITCHES—HOW TO KEEP TRACK?

Let's talk about innings for a minute. I advocate that young pitchers keep their innings thrown down. But a lot of times, especially in professional baseball, you'll hear about pitchers being on a pitch count. Well, what's the difference between being on a pitch count and controlling the number of innings thrown?

My personal preference is to use innings thrown because they're just a little bit easier to track over time. If you're tracking your innings throughout a year, it's a little bit easier to do than to say, "How many pitches have I thrown?" Most of the time, you figure between 20 and 25 pitches in a normal inning. Fifteen pitches is a pristine inning, almost perfect. If you get out of an inning faster than 15 pitches, that's awesome, but most players should figure 20 to 25 pitches per inning.

Given that number, innings are just easier to count. For the guys at my gym, when they come in for their assessment or reassessment every quarter, it's easy for me to say, "Hey, how many innings have you thrown since our last meeting?" versus the number of pitches they've thrown. It's all about total volume on the shoulder. We're just looking for a metric on that, and I think that counting innings is easier than counting pitches. But one is not inherently better than the other. Do what works best for you and your coach.

eral different muscles and can be very individualized. We see a lot of impingement at the hip and torn labrums as well in the baseball population. As with most injuries, the biggest thing is controlling the time out on the field. The hips rotate in a major league baseball player at 700+ degrees per second—that's a ton of torque and strain on a joint—so it's easy to understand how limiting innings can minimize that strain.

The second thing you can do to avoid hip injuries is to address the glaring strength and mobility restrictions in the weight room. Things like basic foam rolling techniques and basic stretching techniques can really help prevent those types of hip injuries. The reason for this is that the sport of baseball is so rotational. Everything you do on a baseball field is rotational. When you throw, you're rotating through your hips. When you hit, you're again rotating through the hips. That's why we see such shortness of the some of the muscles in the hips and down regulation of others: when you're trying to do something so explosively so often in one area of the body, it creates tension in that area and down regulates other muscles. And that's when injuries pop up. So when you can do things in the weight room to balance out that tension, things like different mobility and foam rolling treatments, then you're easily on the path to avoiding hip injuries.

LOWER BACK INJURIES

I'm also seeing a lot of lower back injuries, especially in younger guys. I've even had a couple of guys come to the gym recently who had fractures of the lower back before they were 18 years old. That's just insane to me! Again, overuse plays a huge role in this, but we can also attribute it to improper mechanics on the baseball field and to weakness in the core. Both of these factors are going to play a role in lower back injuries.

These guys come in with a weak core and an over-exaggerated extension posture. They're leaning back. Most of the guys who are very explosive or fast are naturally going to be a little bit extended. But here's what happens—if you're in that posture for a long period of time and then you add rotation of the spine through throwing or hitting on top of that extension posture, you now have the joints of your spine banging up against each other and rotating, creating torque at the spine.

When you rotate, you want to rotate through the hips, like I mentioned above. But when you're in that extension posture, it's a lot harder to keep that rotation only at the hips. Some of the movement is moved up and occurs at the spine. Anytime we have the joints of the spine banging into one another and rotating, that is an absolute recipe for injury at the lower back.

So the number-one thing we can do to help keep players' backs healthy is to improve their anterior core strength, improve their posture, and help lengthen the big muscles of the back—the lats. These three things fit together hand in hand and will take stress off of the discs and lower back.

Coach Showcase: John Oehler

"Appenzeller training is not about just making the athletes strong, but also explosive and agile!"

Appenzeller training has been a great addition to our baseball program. In one season, we doubled our team stolen bases, increased our team batting average, and have become mentally tougher! Coach CJ has made our players stronger and more explosive from all standpoints on the baseball field. Coach CJ brings a work ethic, intensity, and motivation that no other can match, and any focused player looking to play at the next level needs this training. Appenzeller training is not just about making the athletes strong, but also explosive and agile!

—*Coach John Oehler, Head Coach*

West Deptford High School Varsity Baseball

Player Showcase: Dan Valerio

"Training at ATS has given me the opportunity to receive Division I baseball scholarships and a shot at the MLB draft."

From training at ATS, my increase in power is just incredible. This previous summer I hit 26 doubles, which was more than three times as many as I hit in the same amount of games last year. Training has given me the opportunity to receive Division I baseball scholarships and a shot at the MLB draft. Also, my ability to move around at second base has dramatically improved, and I can get to more balls up the middle and deep in the hole. All of these results are just maximizing my full potential on the field and in life. I dominate baseball games now, I don't just participate!!!

Basically, without CJ changing my life, I would be the same headcase ball player I was when I was younger. CJ instilled confidence and integrity in my life. I can honestly say I'm blue collar because CJ showed me what it takes!

My favorite memory at ATS is when CJ closed all the doors on a hot summer day and turned the heat on. This workout was the most intense, most demanding workout I've ever been a part of. But things like that shape you for life. No matter what, you can't quit, even when it gets hard.

—*Dan Valerio*

Rowan College at Gloucester County Baseball

Chapter 3: Strength Training for All Ages

Many parents of young athletes are concerned about strength training, especially regarding *when* they should be doing it. At what age should a young athlete start strength training?

When Do You Start Strength Training?

Strength training is appropriate for any athlete as long as he or she is able to conceptualize the idea of strength training—the idea of getting a little bit better in their sport or of being competitive. That said, you have to make sure the strength training is age appropriate. We have boys as young as nine years old in our facility, and at that age, we're focusing strictly on the fundamentals: mastering bodyweight movements, mastering the push-up, mastering the recline row, mastering the pull-up, doing bodyweight squats and bodyweight lunges. We focus on exercises like that and building stability.

A lot of these movements go directly back to the injury section of this book. We're talking a lot about how that frontal core has a lot to do with preventing injuries, so at a young age, we're focused on building up the frontal core, on building up an athlete's stability, reducing stiffness in that area, and mastering every single movement to absolute perfection.

Before we ever add load or any type of weight to these young athletes, we want to make sure they're ready to go to that next level, that they're ready to add weight. We want to ensure that they are ready to move through a proper range of motion correctly with some weight added. So that's what we're focusing on at a younger level. Again, kids at pretty much any age could start doing some bodyweight movements as long as they're old enough to conceptualize the idea that, "Hey I'm working out so

YOUNG ATHLETES IN TRAINING

Whenever I'm asked what age an athlete can start training, I always remember the youngest athlete to ever train at our facility—his name was Logan, and when he started training with us, he was 10 years old. This was back before we had our youth program, and he would train right alongside our high school and college athletes. I remember telling his dad that I wasn't sure if he was mature enough to grasp what we were doing and if he understood that he was working towards becoming a better baseball player and athlete. Boy, was I wrong! This kid was like a terminator. He would come a half hour early to workouts and stay a half hour late to do extra training, and he always wanted more to do at home. He told me that he was going to be the strongest athlete I'd ever train and that he wouldn't stop until he was. He was a MADMAN. But he taught me that AGE isn't nearly as important as maturity and some young guys can easily grasp training and working hard and learning the blue collar mindset. Logan is now a stand-out middle school athlete in wrestling and baseball.

I can get a little bit better at my sport. I'm working out so I can hit the ball a little farther, with a little more authority. I'm working out so I can run a little faster. I'm working out so I can get to that ground ball in the hole." As soon as they're mature enough to think about that, they're ready to start strength training.

AGE APPROPRIATE

So what exactly does strength training look like for different age groups? I break young athletes down into three age groups. Our youth group is kids aged nine to 12 years old. We call that group "game strong speed." Our second age group is middle school to high school, roughly 13 to 17 years old. After that, we work with college-age athletes, from 18 on up to about 25 years old.

NINE TO TWELVE

For the game strong speed kids, again, we're focusing on bodyweight movements. A workout might start with work on decelerating. It's important for athletes to learn how to stop before they learn how to run faster. It's important that guys learn how to land before they learn how to jump. So we teach them how to land. We teach them how to decelerate. Then the next thing we're going to do is practice our push-ups. Strength is like a skill—the more you practice it, the better you develop it. So we'll practice push-ups, bodyweight squats, bodyweight lunges, and reclining rows, which also use bodyweight. We have those TRX type of handles that they lay back and do rows from. Then we might practice pull-ups or pull-up holds.

Again, stability is key for this age group, so we do a lot of holds, a lot of isometrics where they're just holding the proper position, a lot of pauses in the squats and in the push-ups. Movements like those are going to be key for this age group. And then we move on to our core training, which at this age, is going to be almost all holding. We'll practice holding different positions, like holding in a plank position, which is something almost everybody is familiar with, or holding a side plank or holding an anti-rotational movement. That's the kind of stuff we're going to focus on in a strength workout for the nine-to-12 group, the game strong speed group.

SAMPLE WORKOUT FOR YOUTH

A1. Hop and Stop 4 x 5

A2. Birddog Hold 4 x :20 Each Side

1A. Bodyweight Tempo Squats 5 x 10

1B. Band Pull Aparts 5 x 10 Overhand 10 Underhand

2A. Recline Rowing on Suspension Trainer 4 x 10

2B. Eccentric Focus Push-up 4 x 5

3A. Walking Lunges 3 x 10

3B. Belly Swing 3 x 10

4A. Sled Dragging 3-5 x 110'

THIRTEEN TO SEVENTEEN

For this age group, now we're going to start adding some more dynamic movements. We're going to add some sub-maximum loads and rotational power movements. For example, they would throw medicine balls or throw steel bells against the wall or throw things to each other. We're also going to add lateral power and jumping and sprinting. It's not that we don't sprint with the youth group, but when we do, the focus is on teaching them how to decelerate, how to stop properly, how to change directions properly. When we sprint with the 13-to-17 age group, we're teaching them how to produce more force, how to be more powerful over a given amount of time.

SAMPLE WORKOUT WEEK FOR MIDDLE SCHOOL/ EARLY HIGH SCHOOL

Day 1 – FULL BODY

A1. Box Jump 4 x 3

A2. Core Engaged Deadbug 4 x 3

A3. Band Pull-Apart 4 x 10 Overhand 10 Underhand

1A. Trap Bar Deadlift 3 x 5

1B. Side Plank 3 x :30 Each Side

2A. 1-Arm McGill Dumbbell Bench 4 x 6

2B. Chest Supported Dumbbell Row 4 x 12

3A. Reverse Lunge 3 x 8

3B. Kettlebell Swing 3 x 8

Day 2 – FULL BODY

A1. Medicine Ball Scoop Toss 3 x 5

A2. Bottoms-Up Kettlebell Carry 3 x 55'

A3. Active Release on Traps 3 x :30

1A. Dumbbell Bench 5 x 6-8

1B. Band Pull-Apart 5 x 12

2A. Step-Up 4 x 6

2B. Kettlebell Romanian Deadlift 4 x 12

3A. Chin-Up 3 x Submax

3B. Facepull with External Rotation 3 x 15

4A. Dumbbell Row 3 x 8

4B. Pallof Hold 3 x :30

Day 3 – FULL BODY

A1. Heiden Jump 3 x 3

A2. Medicine Ball Stomp 3 x 6

A3. Suitcase Carry 3 x 55'

1A. Double Kettlebell Rear Foot Elevated Split Squat 4 x 6

1B. Facepull 4 x 12

2A. Landmine Press 4 x 8

2B. Neutral Grip Chin-Ups 4 x Submax

3A. Hip Thrust 3 x 12

3B. Sled Drags 3 x 110'

EIGHTEEN TO TWENTY-FIVE

Finally, when we get to our college guys, our workouts will be very similar to what we do with our middle school and high school guys, but with a little bit more advanced progressions. We might add in things like barbell work and barbell squatting with a safety squat bar. They're adding in barbell deadlifting off the floor. Now that they've gone through our program, they understand stability and they understand the movements, they understand what position they want to be in and what they're trying to do with the bar or what they're trying to do with this certain jump or throw, and it can really produce a lot of force.

SAMPLE WORKOUT WEEK FOR HIGH-LEVEL HIGH SCHOOL/COLLEGE

DAY 1 – Lower Body

A1. Repeated Heiden Jumps 4 x 5

A2. Core Engaged Dead Bug 4 x 5

1A. Sumo Deadlift off a 1" Block 5 Rep Max

1B. Suitcase Carry 3 x 55'

2A. Reverse Lunge 4 x 8/

2B. Thanksgiving Facepull 4 x 15

3A. Kettlebell Romanian Deadlift 3 x 12

3B. Valslide Eccentric Hamstring Curl 3 x 12

DAY 2 – Upper Body

A1. Hot Foot Medicine Ball Scoop Toss 3 x 5

A2. Kettlebell Waiter's Walk 3 x 55'

A3. Active Release on Traps 3 x :30

1A. Recline Rowing with Suspension Trainer 3 x MAX REPS (Technical Failure)

1B. Yoga Pushup 3 x 8

2A. 1-Arm McGill Dumbbell Bench Press 4 x 6

2B. 1-Arm Dumbbell Row 4 x 6

3A. Banded Triple Threat (Facepull + External Rotation + Press) 3 x 12

3B. Scap-Up or Push-Up Plus 3 x 12

DAY 3 – Lower Body

A1. Reactive Seated Box Jump 5 x 3

A2. Pallof Press 3 x 6

1A. Safety Squat Bar Rear foot Elevated Split Squat 3 x 3

1B. Lying Clam 3 x 6

2A. Kettlebell Swing 4 x 8

2B. Single Leg Hip Thurst 4 x 8

2C. Dumbbell Leg Curl ISO Hold 4 x :30

3A. Sled Drag 3-5 x 110'

DAY 4 – Upper Body

A1. Double Clutch Medicine Ball Stomp 3 x 3

A2. Serratus Wall Slide 3 x 6

1A. DB Bench with Fat Grips 5 x 5 + Drop set 1 x 10-15

1B. Band Pull Apart 10 Reps per Set Overhand and Underhand

2A. Landmine Press 4 x 6

2B. Neutral Grip Weighted Chins 4 x 6

3A. Alternating Eccentric Recline Rows 3 x 6

3B. L-Lateral Raise + External Rotation 3 x 12

3C. Hammer Curl 3 x 12

INDIVIDUAL APPROPRIATE

The other thing to know is that individuals vary. Take, for instance, someone in the youth group who has been here a little longer. He might be compatible with an older kid who is just starting out. Look at a young athlete who's 12 years old and moving into the sixth grade but who has been working with me for several years—he's been here and he's good, he has a good idea of movement and stability—and he might be allowed to add an external load. He might be able to add a kettle bell to his squat and do a kettle bell goblet squat.

The same thing goes for a high school athlete. Maybe he's 16 or 17 years old, but he's been with us since he was 10 years old. He's going to be able to add a barbell squat a little bit sooner because, again, he understands stability and movement; he understands what we're trying to accomplish. It's just like in school: you don't go to sixth grade before you learn first-grade math. It's the same thing here. You don't put a bar on your back before you understand how to squat with only your bodyweight, and then with a kettle bell, and then with a sandbag. We have steps, we have a system of progressions and regressions that is set up to make everyone successful, right where they are at this point in time.

BONUS WORKOUT

(For Either Middle School, High School, or College. We implement Movement Days depending on Time of Year/Competitive Calendar.)

Full Dynamic Warm Up

OH Marching 2 x 120'

OH A-Skip 2 x 120'

OH Walking Lunges 2 x 120'

Power Skip 2 x 120'

Lateral Slides 2 x 120'

Power Hip Carioca 2 x 120'

Speed Carioca 2 x 120'

Spiderman Walk 2 x 120'

Overhead Medicine Ball Throw for Distance 4 x 2

10-Yard Pushup Start Sprints x 6 (Arbitrary Rest – Focus on Acceleration Technique)

20 MB Throw Start Sprints x 6 (Minute-and-a-Half Rest)

Player Showcase: Tyler Dixon

"I wasn't slashing the ball anymore, I was DRIVING it, which made me a THREAT in the playoffs!"

Working with CJ has made me physically and mentally a better player and PERSON. Physically, I'm stronger, faster, and more powerful than I've ever been. These things truly translated well right onto the field. Walking into my junior year, I had new arm strength and speed in the outfield that impressed coach and got me in the lineup. The new arm strength even got me on the mound (where I haven't been since I was a kid). When I got my shot to swing, I wasn't slashing the ball anymore: I was driving it, which made me a key component in the playoffs last year.

Not only did the hard work at ATS get bigger and better physically, it also shaped the mental part of my game as well, teaching me to really focus and get everything out of what I do and to get and keep the blue collar mindset and stay part of the one percent.

The system really works, and I can't thank CJ enough for everything he has done for me.

—*Tyler Dixon*

Eastern High School Baseball

OF/P

Parent Showcase: Dalton Hilaman

"He was a dink and dunk kind of hitter, but now he's putting the ball into all areas of the outfield."

Some of the things I have noticed about Dalton in baseball since he started training at ATS are huge. For one thing, you can just tell in how he now approaches a game or practice because he's enjoying the game more due to being better prepared for the hard work that goes into it.

Another thing I have noticed is the better jumps he's getting on the base paths. I'm sure the speed work and leg sleds had a lot to do with it. Dalton has always been quick, but he has had trouble getting started. Since going to the ATS youth speed camps, he's getting faster, larger jumps and stealing more bases. His coach was just telling me the other day that he loves having Dalton on the base path because he causes nothing but havoc to the opposing team.

His batting is also now starting to come around. He is starting to drive the ball farther and more consistently. He was a dink-and-dunk kind of hitter, but now he's putting the ball into all areas of the outfield. He always hated to do push-ups, but now while we're hanging out, he sometimes just gets down and starts doing them.

I remember when he first started to come to ATS, he hated to work hard to the point that he would break down and cry. It really meant a lot to him that you took the time to actually not only push him forward, but also do it with him. He's now running laps at practice with no problems.

—*Dave Hilaman*

Father of Dalton Hilaman

Tribe AAU Baseball

Chapter 4: Baseball and Strength Training

We've talked generally about how strength training can make you a better baseball player and especially how it can prevent injuries, but how is it specifically going to make you better on the field?

Strength training affects nearly every aspect of the game. You're going to see bat speed and explosive power hitting improve. You're going to get more velocity or miles per hour on your arm, definitely. You're going to have greater field speed, which includes getting better jumps on the baseball, covering more ground in the field, and also stealing more bases and being more of a threat on the base pads. And then finally, there's conditioning. You have to realize that all conditioning is not created equal. Being conditioned for baseball is a lot different from, say, being conditioned for a wrestling match or a cross-country event, which is a notion that gets lost sometimes when you're talking about conditioning. Being "baseball conditioned" means being able to play a 14-inning double header at the high school level or play a nine-inning game when you get to your first year of college. So all of these are facets of the game that are affected by strength training.

Bat Speed

One way to improve bat speed is to improve the player's actual swing from a mechanics standpoint. A hitting coach can improve someone's swing. That's not what we do at my facility, though. That's the job of a skill coach. What we do here is to improve a player's core strength first of all. We work on rotational strength through their trunk so we can improve the rate at which they swing or the speed at which they swing and rotate their trunk around. We do this through movements like explosive medicine ball throws, for example.

Another way to work on bat speed with strength training is to increase a player's lower body strength. A lot of guys say, "Oh, you hit with your legs, you hit with your legs." Well, that's true to a certain degree. The more strength you have in the lower body and the harder you can drive with your hips, then the more force ultimately you're going to be able to place into the baseball.

And then finally, I would say that the rotational aspect is huge. We can improve the mobility and the ability to rotate through a full range of motion at a high speed in the weight room. That's going to allow you to hit the ball farther with more velocity, go gap to gap a little bit better, and probably hit more home runs and more doubles.

VELOCITY

The most important way that strength training helps improve velocity is by strengthening the rotator cuff. I want athletes to think of the rotator cuff as the brakes. The internal rotators of your shoulder are already plenty strong. You've been throwing a baseball for a long time, so these muscles are already developed. But they'll only accelerate to the speed at which you can decelerate. They'll only go as fast as you can slow down with your posterior rotator cuff. It's almost like being in a Ferrari. You don't get in a Ferrari with Ford brakes. Now, that's nothing against Ford brakes, but Ford brakes stop a car that's going 130 miles an hour at most. Ferraris need something that stops 210. So a Ferrari is not going to go 210 miles an hour with Ford brakes in it. Our number-one priority is to build the brakes, which is going to allow you to unlock some of that potential you already have in your arm. It's going to allow you to move your arm faster because your body recognizes, "Wow, I can slow down a little bit faster. I'm going to go a little bit faster now because I can slow down."

Number two, strength training is going to improve your scapular function. Remember from the chapter on injuries that the scapula is your shoulder blade and that the shoulder blade has to go through a certain range of motion in order for your arm to get in a good position to throw really hard. Through strength training, we can increase that range of motion and we can strengthen the smaller muscles that rotate the shoulder blade and put it in a good position to throw. A better position is always going to be equivalent to more velocity.

Those two things I think are key: building the brakes, number one, and improving the function of the shoulder blade, number two. A third factor is lateral power. I talked a little about this in the injury chapter, that throwing is almost like jumping off one leg sideways, or laterally. If you can improve your lower body power in that direction, ultimately you can get your lower body behind your throws driving you toward your target, which is ultimately going to unlock more velocity as well.

FIELD SPEED AND AGILITY

Reaction time is the number-one key to field speed and agility. The way you build reaction time in the weight room is through adding reactive means. Once guys are ready to do explosive movements—once they understand stability and they understand movement—we'll teach them how to add a reactive component to those explosive exercises. These are things like sprinting on command or changing direction on command. These reactive movements improve the reaction time of the athlete, but we're also bridging the gap from the weight room to the sports field. You're never going to be able to do anything inside a weight room that's identical to what you do on a baseball field. You can't throw a baseball in the weight room. You can't swing a heavier bat to make you swing faster or harder. But you can bridge that gap with some of these reactive components. So the first key to field speed and agility is to get guys more reactive.

Second, we can improve their top speed and their ability to accelerate. And I think in this case that acceleration is more important. A lot of times on the baseball field, if you're playing a game, you're only getting two, three, or four steps. You're never running more than, say, 10 yards. Even that would be really far to run to go get a ball, so really what's important is that first step, that ability to accelerate fast.

That first step has to be aggressive and explosive, and there are two ways to increase a player's ability to unlock quickness on that first step and have them accelerate quickly: number one is by increasing their maximal strength, and number two is by increasing their explosive power. That's how we increase field speed as far as defensive skills go.

Offensively, again, we look at that first step—the next base is only 90 feet away. No one reading this book is ever going to reach top speed at 90 feet; however, our acceleration is where we can make big changes. If a player can cover 20 feet faster than he did before, then he's going to be able to steal more bases. How many games do you watch on TV in which stolen bases are decided by the way the guy slides, which direction, how high the throw is from the catcher? That margin of error is so small that if we can just make guys one step faster, be a little bit more explosive because they got a little bit stronger and a little bit more explosive off their jump, then they're going to steal more bases successfully. And that's how the weight room contributes to field speed and agility.

CONDITIONING

Conditioning is a hot topic in baseball. I think it's sort of like strength training—a coach's idea about conditioning is just passed down from generation to generation to generation. Your coach's coach's coach had his pitchers run poles, so now our pitchers run poles. What I think the most important thing people have to understand is that baseball is not an aerobic sport, so running long distance isn't necessarily going to be beneficial for a baseball player. It might not be a big detriment early on—a little bit of aerobic capacity is good and will help guys recover faster in between games. But ultimately, repeated efforts at high speed are what baseball is about.

So a pitcher throws a pitch, and he has plenty of time in between pitches. What he has to be able to do is throw again just as hard as the last time. He has to be able to sustain his velocity or sustain his power over time, so when we're talking about conditioning for baseball, we're not necessarily talking about going for a long run. We might, as I mentioned, do a little aerobic conditioning in the off-season, especially in the early off-season, but as we get closer and closer to the season, we're going to be doing more and more repeated explosive efforts—more and more repeated explosive medicine ball throws, more and more repeated explosive lateral jumps. Again, we're bridging the gap from the weight room to the field. We're being more specific in the way that players have to be conditioned, to be explosive over time, over multiple bouts. That's conditioning for baseball players in a nutshell. Not all conditioning is created equal.

Player Showcase: Pete Bernato

"If it weren't for CJ, I wouldn't be playing college baseball because I wouldn't have the confidence to get back on the field and be successful."

ATS has helped me in more than one way. I was a very injury-prone player, and I tore my ACL and ripped apart my ankle. Both required major surgeries that took an extensive time to get back on the field. The physical training at ATS for me was focused on turning my physical weaknesses into strengths, and in the end, that made me a stronger person than ever before. I went into ATS weighing about 190, just a tall, lanky kid. By the end of the summer working out three days a week with CJ, I weighed in at 225. It was a solid 225. I felt overall that I was just in completely better shape than I had ever been and that I was able to move better than I ever had before.

The mental training at ATS is what allowed me to get back on the field after my ankle surgery and be a better player than I was before. At ATS, it's more than just lifting weights; it is destroying your goals and working toward your dreams. CJ teaches you how to push through the pain and appreciate the grind, because in the end, if you do both of those things, you will the best you can be at all things you do in life. It if weren't for CJ, I wouldn't be playing college baseball because I wouldn't have the confidence to get back on the field and be successful.

—*Pete Bernato*

Wilmington University Baseball

Parent Showcase: Nick DiBlasi

"CJ has made our son stronger and healthier not just in his body but in his mind."

My son Nick has been training with CJ for almost a year now, and the transition we have seen is unbelievable. First and foremost, Nick has become so much stronger and faster than he was only a year ago. Nick was unable to do a pull-up, and a year later, he is able to do sets of six. He trained elsewhere before but was never able to accomplish that and was never happy with trainers. But CJ is a whole different approach to fitness and health, and my son is hooked. CJ's motivation and knowledge is undeniable, and he knows how to make it fun!!! He makes you feel like family, and he cares about each and every person in his gym.

The transformation in Nick's body is unbelievable. Many people have noticed and commented on how his body has changed and how strong he has gotten. Although Nick is only 14, he never misses his sessions with CJ. He is always ready to go and always wants to be early. He comes out of his sessions sweaty and dirty, but he absolutely loves going. I cannot believe this is the same kid!!!! He has even encouraged some of his friends to join training with CJ.

Now, regarding his nutrition changes—this is probably the most amazing to me. Nick always liked his junk food, and I am not saying this boy doesn't have a pizza or a piece of cake now and then, but CJ has changed his whole outlook on eating. Nick eats a good breakfast every day, along with vitamins, and we also pack his lunch with nutritious food versus the crap he used to buy at school every day. When Nick goes to the store, he is now checking labels for sugar content and fat, and he know what foods he now needs to eat to stay fit and healthy. He makes good choices. He no longer drinks soda, mostly water or milk, and he brings a protein shake to every workout to have afterwards. He also drinks those protein shakes at home when he doesn't have time for a snack or breakfast and is eating fruits and salads. His eating habits have completely changed. This to me is astounding for a 14-year-old boy, all credit going to CJ!!!!

CJ has made our son stronger and healthier, not just in his body but in his mind. Nick has a hectic schedule between his sports, his school, and his training sessions, but he is able to handle it as he has become very physically fit. Nick makes sure he gets proper rest. CJ is always teaching him something about getting healthy, being fit, or just giving him words of inspiration, which has given Nick more confidence and has made him feel better about himself. Thank you, CJ—you truly are the best!!!!

—*Gina DiBlasi*

Mother of Nick DiBlasi

Cherokee Baseball

CHAPTER 5: THE RIGHT KIND OF STRENGTH TRAINING

So, let's start to put this all together. Am I simply saying, "Hey, go lift weights"? No, absolutely not. But how do you know if you're getting the right kind of training? If you're a parent, a coach, or an athlete, what does the right kind of training look like?

THE WRONG KIND OF TRAINING

The first way you know that you're receiving the wrong baseball strength training is if it's not specifically individualized for you. Every baseball player, just like every person on the planet, is a little bit different and needs slightly different things from training. For the most part, yes, general strength training can work for everyone. But some of the baseball-specific training, like scapula (shoulder blade) health, can be a little bit different for everybody. Rotator cuff training is going to be a little bit different for everybody. So if that piece of the puzzle, that individual training for each athlete, is missing, then it's probably not great baseball strength training.

Another telltale sign is that an athlete is doing some exercises that baseball players should never do. I'm going to name some specific movements that baseball players should simply never do:

- *The barbell bench press.* As popular as the bench press is—somebody is always asking, "How much do you bench?"—barbell bench pressing for a baseball player is something I would never recommend. It puts the shoulder in a position that athletes already hang out in that internally rotating position, and it's adding load in a compromised position. We've already talked about how often shoulders are injured. Now, with the bench press, you're adding load to an already compromised position. That's definitely not good.

- *Dips.* I would never do dips with a baseball player. Again, this has to do with shoulder health. If you look at the shoulder, it's a ball and socket joint. When you do dips, you're having that ball roll forward in the socket and put a lot of strain on the anterior side or the front side of the shoulder.

- *Overhead barbell press.* Once more, this movement relates to shoulder health. The way the shoulder moves into the shoulder socket doing this exercise creates strain on the rotator cuff, as well as little micro-tears in the rotator cuff, and athletes already get plenty of that just from throwing. We don't want to add to that with our strength training.

- *Squatting with a straight bar.* This is the last specific exercise that I'll mention. I talked earlier about squatting with a safety squat bar, but squatting with a straight bar endangers shoulder health. When you use a safety bar, you're taking the shoulder out of that externally rotated position with a load and putting it in a more advantageous position to keep the shoulder healthy and safe. Squatting with a straight bar has more risk than reward.

Remember, you're not getting great baseball strength training if there's no part of the routine that is individualized for you. If there's no part of your arm care program that is individual to you, and your coach is just saying, "Here is everybody's arm care program," then that's not going to be much good. And second, if you're doing something that's definitely an exercise that baseball players shouldn't even be doing, like the ones I went over above, then you are probably not getting good baseball strength training.

So What Is the Right Kind?

When you're getting the proper baseball strength training, you will have an individualized plan. No two athletes are exactly alike, and you should be doing at least part of your routine that is unique to you. Beyond that, you will be doing specific movements that are on a strength training program designed for baseball players. If you're doing these two things, then you're on the right track.

The right strength training movements for baseball players include:

- *Rotational medicine ball throwing.* Take a medicine ball and throw it rotationally; if you think of your swing, this motion is almost like that. So if you're doing some sort of rotational strength training like that, you're on the right track.

- *Push-ups and push-up variations.* If you're doing a lot of push-up variations and a lot of core training, meaning resisting motion at your midsection—planks are the easiest movement for people to visualize—that's a good indicator. Anything like a plank in which you have to remain neutral over time is good for baseball. As we mentioned, barbell pressing doesn't help you, so replace pressing with push-up variations, and they can even be loaded, like we might load guys with chains for push-ups. We might make push-ups harder by adding a leg lift or something like that. A lot of push-ups are a good indicator that you're in a good baseball strength training program.

- *Lots of pulling.* This would include dumbbell rows, recline rows, and chin-ups. I think a lot of pulling is very advantageous to the baseball player, especially when it's done correctly. It improves that scapular function, that's the shoulder blade function, which is so important in overhead throwing. It also builds on those "breaks" we talked about in improving velocity through strength training.

- *Rotator cuff work.* The last piece of good baseball strength training includes rotator cuff work. The flip side is that *too much* rotator cuff is often not a good thing. Not everything you do should be rotator cuff work, so not everything you do should be a band external rotation or a band exercise.

Player Showcase: Corey Kreston

"Going into my junior year I was high 70s off the mound and not pitching much. Fast forward to now, I'm throwing consistently in the rotation at my high school and sitting at 82 to 84 mph."

Training here at ATS has truly changed my baseball career. First and foremost, I can finally refer to myself as one of the bigger guys on the team. I've always been tall and lanky, but now I have a little bit of muscle on my frame and the strength and power to back up my speed. Since beginning training here at ATS, I've become a power THREAT in the batter's box and go gap to gap with ease. This past summer, I hit near .500 for my Legion team and finished third in the district in batting average.

My arm strength is where I've really seen the hard work I put in here at ATS pay off, though. Going into my junior year, I was high 70s off the mound and not pitching much. Fast forward to now, I'm throwing consistently in the rotation at my high school and sitting at 82 to 84 mph. This year from shortstop, I even hit 87 across the diamond!

I can't thank CJ, ATS, and the blue collar mindset enough for the changes it has made to my game.

—*Corey Kreston*

Eastern High School Baseball

Parent Showcase: Tyler Collins

"… a kid that was a solid contact hitter that slapped the ball to the right and notched base hits up the middle started ripping line drives down the left field line."

My son Tyler Collins has been a solid baseball player from 8U on up to up to 12U. He has been on travel and showcase teams alike. With the new transition to the 60/90 field, we decided to sign Tyler up with the ATS program to add strength in his arm to make the longer throws from short.

What we didn't know and learned after a few months at ATS

was that Tyler's eye–hand coordination had gotten faster—a kid that was a solid contact hitter that slapped the ball to the right and notched base hits up the middle started ripping line drives down the left field line.

Hoping to see strength in his throws, I watched as he started getting more lateral to ground balls up the middle and turning ridiculous backhand plays in deep short with the confidence to make strong throws from everywhere on the field.

His appearance from working out at ATS the last year has changed the way he carries himself as well. More confidence and slight arrogance has replaced a meager personality. He wants to be the best, so he continues to be trained by the best as he enters high school.

—*Fran Collins*

Father of Tyler Collins

Pine Hill Rams Baseball

Chapter 6: The Blue Collar Mindset

The Blue Collar Mindset is something we talk about constantly that is unique to my gym. It's a way of thinking that I created to put into words our approach to training and life. It is very near and dear to my heart, and it's something that everybody who trains here knows about and can talk about. So what is the Blue Collar Mindset?

The Blue Collar Mindset embodies two core principles. Number one: failure is never fatal. Any time we fail, it's simply an opportunity to learn. You can fail in school on a pop quiz or a test. You can fail on the field by striking out, making an error, kicking a ball in the outfield, kicking a ball in the infield, whatever it may be. Or you can fail in the weight room. Not getting an exercise right the first time, going a little bit too heavy, going a little bit too light, doing something that maybe wasn't what we were looking for—those are simply opportunities to learn the right way to do something.

Failure doesn't define us as a person. It doesn't define our success, and it doesn't define where we're going. It's simply an opportunity to learn and grow. Our guys actually get a little bit excited when they fail; it's awesome to see. But they don't say they "failed." They tell me, "Dude, I'm so excited that I messed up" whatever it was, this new double play, this new trick play, "because now I learned and I'll never forget."

The second principle of the Blue Collar mindset says that anything is possible through hard work. Take me—I've been the underdog my whole life. Everything I've ever done, I've been told, "You'll never do this, you'll never do that. It's not realistic. Be more of this, be more of that." And truly, our guys, a lot of them—especially when we first started—were the underdog guys. Even still now, we have a ton of guys that were JV players as juniors or got cut from their freshman team in high school. And I just tell them, consistently, that anything we want to do, whether it's in school, in life, on the baseball field, in the classroom, whatever it is, it is possible through hard work. And those are the two core principles of the Blue Collar Mindset.

WHY THE BLUE COLLAR MINDSET IS IMPORTANT FOR ATHLETES

I think it's so important for guys to have this mindset because in today's world, it just too common to be negative. It's too common to say things and do things that are negative and that don't show respect and love for one another. I think when we're living this Blue Collar Mindset and we're learning from our failures and we're not letting them define us, it just sets us apart. It makes us the one percent of the population that's willing to do it a little bit differently.

I also think that too many people preach reality. "Be realistic, be realistic." So many of our guys have told their teachers their goals. Maybe they've said, "Oh, I want to be a professional baseball player," and their teachers—without ever seeing them play an inning of baseball—tell them, "Be more realistic. What do you really want to do?" I think that's a poor way to approach your life. Truly, I think you can do anything that you want to do if you're willing to do the work.

The problem is that people don't want to do the work for themselves so they preach reality to everyone else. So I think those two things are so important. That's why everyone has to live this kind of mindset. Possibility is really everywhere we look, but we have to be able to do what's necessary.

One guy who jumps out at me is our buddy Dan who trains here. He's a JuCo (junior college) guy. Dan was a good high school player, but not the caliber of player that he is now. I want to say he's an All-American this year at the junior college level. He plays at the number-two junior college in the nation, and he went to high school in the North Jersey area. Out of high school, he had zero college offers. Now, this is a kid who is going to play potentially at the best junior college in the nation. He has six Division I offers. He has major league teams following his every move, and he has the opportunity to play at the major league level—and as a high school player, he couldn't even get an offer to a college.

So Dan is a guy who stands out in my mind. He's constantly texting me, asking me for other little things to do. He's the type of guy you tell, "Okay, listen, eat breakfast," and he texts you a picture of his breakfast. "Okay, Dan, drink a protein shake," and he texts you a picture of his protein shake. Then he asks, "What else should I put in here?" Guys like Dan inspire me to keep this thing going, number one, and number two, he sets the example for our younger guys that come in. He can say, "Listen, this is what's possible. When I was your age, I had nothing going for me. When I was a freshman in high school, I played freshman baseball, and now I'm one of the top players in the nation at the junior college level," so it's pretty inspiring stuff.

BUYING IN TO THE BLUE COLLAR MINDSET

Every single parent, especially of the younger kids, they notice this Blue Collar Mindset. Some of them can't label it or put their finger on what it is, but they all notice it. Our guys, what they do when they start training and they really buy into the program, they become more explosive, they become faster. Their performance on the field absolutely goes up.

But that's not all. What we also notice is that the things they do at home go through the roof, like, for instance, their nutrition. They're increasing the amount of great food they eat. They're eating off our shopping list, and they're doing some of the little things that maybe their parents could never get them to do before. Another thing is their studies in school. Almost every single person we work with sees his grades go up. We have a minimum GPA requirement at the facility. Every single person we train has not only reached that minimum, but far exceeded it. Every single one of them sees the grades go up because they take this Blue Collar Mindset into everything, not just into their training. Now at school, they're saying, "Man, I failed that, I'm going to come back and learn from that. How do I get better? How do I work harder so this never happens again?"

And finally, we definitely see the swagger. When they step on the field, they're more confident. All the parents tell me how much more confident their kids are because they know that they put in the work in the off-season and in the in-season. When everybody else is playing video games and hanging out, they were putting in the extra stuff that made the difference. That's what we hear from parents and coaches. Coaches of teams we have worked with have told us that, first off, the overall swagger of the team has improved, and second, leaders emerge on their teams through the training. When they go through the training, the guys that buy in immediately emerge as leaders to kind of push the entire team to buy into the mindset, to buy the work ethic and to buy into doing the little things that are necessary to be great.

Player Showcase: Ryan Keen

"As a junior, I had a dominating season that finished with me in the starting lineup for the Carpenter Cup. I hit four homeruns (I'd only EVER hit two before training at ATS), hit .375 on varsity (the year before, I hit .250 on JV), and was top 10 in South Jersey in doubles."

Heading into my junior year of baseball at Eastern, I had no idea what the future held for me. I was way down on the depth chart for varsity, and I knew my coach wouldn't keep me to play JV (like I did last year) as a junior. As my fall ball season wrapped up, I began looking for the best way to improve my game physically and mentally, and one of my teammates told me about CJ and ATS. The rest is history: over my time at ATS, I've lost about 30 pounds, taken 0.7 off my 60, and I MADE VARSITY.

However, the results from my training here at ATS didn't stop there—when I got my chance on the field, I made it count. As a junior, I had a dominating season that finished with me in the starting lineup for the Carpenter Cup. I hit four homeruns (I'd only EVER hit two before training at ATS), hit .375 on varsity (the year before I hit .250 on JV), and was top 10 in South Jersey in doubles.

Oh, I almost forgot to mention: I recently committed to Alvernia University to live out my life-long dream of playing college baseball.

Thank you, CJ, and thank you, ATeam!

—*Ryan Keen*

Alvernia University Baseball

Player Showcase: PJ Tome

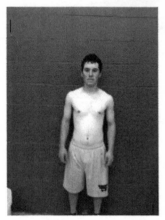

"I've gained 50 pounds of muscle. I'm throwing harder, I've increased my bat speed, and I'm quicker on the base path."

Ever since I started working out at ATS, I have become both physically and mentally stronger. CJ has pushed me to my limits multiple times, and it motivates me to keep pushing and doing my best with everything I do, both in the gym and on the baseball field.

I have gained 50 pounds of muscle in the two years that I have been training at ATS, but putting on the solid weight wasn't the end of the results I have experienced from training here. I also noticed changes on the baseball field: I am throwing a lot harder, my bat speed has gone up tremendously, and I am now able to hit the ball a lot further. I also noticed that I have gotten a lot quicker running the bases.

Ever since I began training here at ATS and developing more strength and explosive power, my batting average has been increasing every year and allowing me to get more playing time.

ATS has given me the strength that I needed to be successful in my baseball career.

—*PJ Tome*

Hammonton High School Baseball

Parent Showcase: Michael Castellano

"He has gone from a singles hitter to driving the ball for extra base hits. We attribute this directly to his training at ATS."

We are so thrilled that our son, Michael (aka MAC), is training with CJ and his staff at Appenzeller Training Systems (ATS).

MAC plays baseball and soccer on travel teams and for his school. MAC started training at ATS in October 2014. For the March to July 2015 school and travel baseball season, MAC has improved dramatically. Being a lead-off hitter, he has been counted on to get on base any way he can, and he carried a batting average of .641 as well as a high on-base percentage that led his teams for the entire season. He has gone from a singles hitter to driving the ball for extra-base hits. We account this directly to his training at ATS. He has gained strength, agility, and confidence, which has helped him succeed this past baseball season. It is obvious that Mac has become much stronger with the workouts.

MAC's soccer season thus far has shown increased strength behind his kicks, and his speed has improved dramatically. Although he is smaller, he is no long intimidated or physically outplayed by anyone. He consistently beats everyone on his freshman team in the mile run and is constantly lowering his time!

CJ also instills proper nutrition in all his athletes. He gives them guides to eating proper types of food for nutrition. He explains needing an increased amount of food for proper fueling of the body; eating multiple times per day to obtain enough calories; incorporating protein to assist with muscle-building; and drinking water for proper hydration. Because MAC looks up to CJ and trusts him, this has assisted me in helping MAC improve his eating and drinking habits for better nutrition.

From his training and better nutrition, MAC's physique has changed, showing muscles and being toned in various areas of his body. What 14-year-old boy wouldn't want that?!

CJ also recognized MAC's effort and determination to make his workouts be effective regardless if he was sore or tired. MAC won an award from CJ at his "Appy Awards" for this achievement. It is obvious how much CJ cares about all of his athletes and how much he wants them to succeed for their personal well-being. That being said, we are so thankful to have met CJ and joined his program.

—*Deborah Castellano*

Mother of Michael Castellano

Cherokee High School Baseball

Client Showcase: Nick Roesch

"On the mound, he has added a few MPH to his fastball and his arm no longer gets sore after a long outing."

We can't say enough fantastic things about CJ Appenzeller's ATS training program.

Nick experienced many pains and muscle soreness associated from the daily grind of playing baseball; especially with a heavy work load of pitching. Based on a friends recommendation, Nick started training twice a week at a gym that specialized in training for athletes. After a year of training at the prior facility, we did see Nick progress. However, the rate of progression was not what we would expect from training two times a week over a year. We saw him sitting around waiting between exercises and reps more than actually exercising. The facility seemed more invested in getting a financial commitment from the families rather than the athlete's development and goals.

From the first minute of the class he was hooked! CJ connects with each person that attends his classes and motivates each one differently. After his first training class, Nick was pumped up to go back for another class. Nick looks forward to coming to every training session; CJ has created an exceptional environment for athletes to train and hang out.

Since training with CJ, we have seen his muscle mass, strength, speed and confidence grow significantly, much more than his previous gym, in only 5 months. His muscle mass gain is obvious, he has developed muscle and visually looks like an athlete; he is no longer that skinny tall kid. I noticed his strength and speed increases during the most recent Fall Baseball season. At the plate, Nick has been driving the baseball in the outfield an additional 15-20 feet. On the mound, he has added a few MPH to his fastball and his arm no longer gets sore after a long outing. The most unexpected improvement has been his speed.

CONCLUSION

Baseball players often catch a bad rap for being "non-athletes" - if you've ever laced up a pair of spikes you know that that is NOT the case.

We have to start approaching strength training for baseball the same way we approach our skill work for baseball, with a serious conviction to improve just like any other athlete would.

Baseball is more competitive today than ever before, YOU can't get left in the dust. You can't just roll up to the field throw your glove on and jog out onto the dirt anymore, at least not if you want to reach a high level. Do what is NECCESARY to stay ahead of the curve.

Strength training will keep you ahead of the curve, healthy, and performing at your best. Just like anything else the amount of time, energy, and effort you put in will provide your cumulative result - take it SERIOUS and adopt the Blue Collar Mindset. Be the work horse not the show horse out on the field, in the gym, and in the cage. Anything you want to accomplish in this game is possible, but you have to WORK for it.

Strength training has transformed my life in more ways then one and it has the power to do the same for your athletic career and life if you buy in. I implore you to adopt a program for yourself and execute.

As with anything in the game of baseball you want to improve in, utilize an expert coaches help - someone who understands the unique needs of the game and will support you every step of the way.

If your not sure if you should start strength training to improve your performance, get out of the dark ages! Strength training the right way has taken hundreds of thousands of ballplayers performance to new heights. It changes ballplayers ability to reach high levels and their mindsets weekly at our small gym in South Jersey, let it work for YOU too.

ABOUT THE AUTHOR

CJ Appenzeller is a strength coach and gym owner located in West Berlin, NJ who specializes in the training of baseball athletes from the youth ranks up and through the college ranks and beyond. CJ specializes in training baseball athletes to not only improve physically but also mentally by helping his athletes develop into world-class athletes and people. He is widely regarded by the coaches, players, and parents that he works with as the most caring and dedicated strength coach / trainer that they have ever worked with and is known for going the extra mile in developing and supporting his athletes and being a role model to them inside and outside of the gym walls.

CJ began his path in strength and conditioning in middle school when he realized his moderate level of talent for the game of baseball would not carry him to the heights in the game he aspired to reach. CJ was told as an 8th grader that he would never make the baseball team at his high school, as there were "a lot of talented players trying out and he did nothing above average." That lit a fire in him to do the one thing he knew he could do above average – work extremely HARD. He was introduced to strength training by his Uncle Chas at the age of twelve and immediately saw that with training and work ethic anything was possible.

After multiple injuries ended CJ's career in college baseball he decided it was time to focus all of his energy into his true passion – helping other players develop into stronger versions of themselves and helping the underdog ballplayer become the standout.

Beyond the X's and O's of training CJ is ultra passionate about instilling and spreading the message of his coined way of thinking and approaching all things in life: The Blue Collar Mindset which has two core principles that fit right in with everything CJ has done up and until this point:

1. Failure is Never Fatal

and

2. Anything is possible through hard work.

If you'd like to learn more about CJ you can reach him at atsstrength@gmail.com

* Free Gift *

Thank you for reading this book. As a reward for you, we'd like to share with you a free gift. When you reference this book and call 856-534-0822 you will receive a complimentary introductory workout as well as a full assessment ($97 value) for FREE!

Made in the USA
San Bernardino, CA
21 December 2016